Little People, **BIG DREAMS**™

MALALA YOUSAFZAI

Written by
Maria Isabel Sánchez Vegara

Illustrated by
Manal Mirza

Frances Lincoln
Children's Books

In the beautiful Swat Valley, in Pakistan, lived a Muslim girl called Malala. Her home was humble, and so was the school for girls her father ran. Malala couldn't wait to grow up, attend class and discover all her talents.

Even though education is every human's right, her mother never had the chance to learn how to read and write. Still, Malala hoped her life would be different. She wanted to prove to everyone that girls can have big dreams, too.

But Malala's dream became a nightmare when a violent group called the Taliban took control of her valley. They banned most of the things she liked, from listening to music, to taking photographs, and even flying kites.

The Taliban believed that, instead of going to school, girls should get married, cover their bodies from head to toe, and never leave the house without their husbands or brothers. It was like being in prison for doing nothing wrong!

In just a heartbeat, the Taliban destroyed hundreds of all-girls schools and made parents scared to send their daughters to class. Malala and the rest of the students wondered what they could do to stop the madness.

Maybe the Taliban had bombs and guns, but Malala and her friends had books and pens to fight back with.

They decided to raise their voices and speak up about how important it was for their future to attend school.

They shared their story on local television, and soon, Malala was asked to write a diary about her life under Taliban rule for the BBC. She used the name of a heroine from one of her favorite Pashtun tales, "Gul Makai."

But for the Taliban, there was nothing scarier than a girl willing to speak up. One day, Malala and two of her friends were shot on their way back home from school. Malala was very badly injured.

The whole world cried for her.

When Malala woke up, she couldn't recognize her room. She had been taken to a hospital in England, far away from home. But children all over the world had written get well wishes. There was a pile of letters waiting to be read!

Malala did not just get better, but stronger and louder.
She knew her story was the story of millions of other girls,
too. With her father's help, she created a foundation
to improve their lives and their education.

Two years later, she became the youngest person ever to receive the Nobel Peace Prize.

Malala brought with her some brave friends from Pakistan,
Nigeria, and Syria, who deserved the same recognition.

From the White House to refugee camps, Malala traveled the world, speaking up about every child's right to go to school.

But as soon as she was settled in her new home
in England, it was time for her to attend class.

The day she received her degree from the University of Oxford was one of her happiest. Still, the next morning, she woke up ready to fight for all the little Malalas in the world and their right to dream as big as they want.

And she will keep doing so.

MALALA YOUSAFZAI

(Born 1997)

2009

2013

Malala Yousafzai was born in 1997, in an area of Pakistan called Swat Valley. Her father was an educator who taught at schools and other learning centers. Before she could even talk, Malala would wander into his classes—and pretend to be the teacher! Her family taught her that education is precious, and as she got older, she became more and more passionate about a child's right to go to school. When Malala was 10 years old, a group known as the Taliban took power in the region she called home. They set out new, strict rules, including a ban on dancing, television, and—most devastating of all—girls going to school. When people spoke against them, the Taliban used violence and fear to get their way. Hundreds of schools were destroyed. But even though she was afraid, Malala saw

2013   2019

that guns and bombs were useless against a girl with pens and books. She decided to stand up for what she believed in. On Pakistani TV and with the BBC, Malala spoke out against the crime of denying girls an education. Suddenly, it was the Taliban's turn to be afraid. Malala was shot by them in 2012, on the bus home from school. Miraculously, she recovered—and got back to campaigning for a girl's right to education. This time, the world listened. She spoke at the United Nations, met refugees and other activists, and became a champion for the rights of children the world over. Malala is the youngest person ever to receive the Nobel Peace Prize, and today continues to campaign for a child's right to a future as big and bright as their dreams.

Want to find out more about **Malala Yousafzai?**

Read these great books:

Malala's Magic Pencil by Malala Yousafzai and Kerascoët

Malala: My Story of Standing Up for Girls' Rights by Malala Yousafzai and Patricia McCormick

Brimming with creative inspiration, how-to projects, and useful information to enrich your everyday life, Quarto Knows is a favorite destination for those pursuing their interests and passions. Visit our site and dig deeper with our books into your area of interest: Quarto Creates, Quarto Cooks, Quarto Homes, Quarto Lives, Quarto Drives, Quarto Explores, Quarto Gifts, or Quarto Kids.

Text © 2021 Maria Isabel Sánchez Vegara. Illustrations © Manal Mirza 2021.
Original concept of the series by Maria Isabel Sánchez Vegara, published by Alba Editorial, s.l.u
Produced under trademark licence from Alba Editorial s.l.u and Beautifool Couple S.L.
First Published in the US in 2021 by Frances Lincoln Children's Books, an imprint of The Quarto Group.
Quarto Boston North Shore, 100 Cummings Center, Suite 265D, Beverly, MA 01915, USA
Tel: +1 978-282-9590, Fax: +1 978-283-2742 **www.QuartoKnows.com**

A catalogue record for this book is available from the British Library.
ISBN 978-0-7112-5904-1
Set in Futura BT.

Published by Katie Cotton • Designed by Sasha Moxon
Edited by Katy Flint • Production by Nikki Ingram
Editorial Assistance from Alex Hithersay
Manufactured In China CC122020
1 3 5 7 9 8 6 4 2

Photographic acknowledgements (pages 28-29, from left to right): 1. Malala Yousafzai, 12, lives in the Swat Valley with her family, pictured on March 26, 2009 © Veronique de Viguerie/Getty Images. 2. Pakistani student Malala Yousafzai speaks to the media at UN headquarters in New York, 2013 © STAN HONDA/AFP via Getty Images. 3. Malala Yousafzai opens the new Library of Birmingham at Centenary Square on September 3, 2013 in Birmingham, England © Christopher Furlong/Getty Images 4. Nobel Peace Prize laureate Malala Yousafzai poses for photo session during the G7 Development and Education Ministers Meeting, in Paris, 2019 © CHRISTOPHE PETIT TESSON/AFP via Getty Images.

Collect the Little People, BIG DREAMS™ series:

FRIDA KAHLO

ISBN: 978-1-84780-783-0

COCO CHANEL

ISBN: 978-1-84780-784-7

MAYA ANGELOU

ISBN: 978-1-84780-889-9

AMELIA EARHART

ISBN: 978-1-84780-888-2

AGATHA CHRISTIE

ISBN: 978-1-84780-960-5

MARIE CURIE

ISBN: 978-1-84780-962-9

ROSA PARKS

ISBN: 978-1-78603-018-4

AUDREY HEPBURN

ISBN: 978-1-78603-053-5

EMMELINE PANKHURST

ISBN: 978-1-78603-020-7

ELLA FITZGERALD

ISBN: 978-1-78603-087-0

ADA LOVELACE

ISBN: 978-1-78603-076-4

JANE AUSTEN

ISBN: 978-1-78603-120-4

GEORGIA O'KEEFFE

ISBN: 978-1-78603-122-8

HARRIET TUBMAN

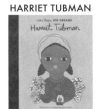

ISBN: 978-1-78603-227-0

ANNE FRANK

ISBN: 978-1-78603-229-4

MOTHER TERESA

ISBN: 978-1-78603-230-0

JOSEPHINE BAKER

ISBN: 978-1-78603-228-7

L. M. MONTGOMERY

ISBN: 978-1-78603-233-1

JANE GOODALL

ISBN: 978-1-78603-231-7

SIMONE DE BEAUVOIR

ISBN: 978-1-78603-232-4

MUHAMMAD ALI

ISBN: 978-1-78603-331-4

STEPHEN HAWKING

ISBN: 978-1-78603-333-8

MARIA MONTESSORI

ISBN: 978-1-78603-755-8

VIVIENNE WESTWOOD

ISBN: 978-1-78603-757-2

MAHATMA GANDHI

ISBN: 978-1-78603-787-9

DAVID BOWIE

ISBN: 978-1-78603-332-1

WILMA RUDOLPH

ISBN: 978-1-78603-751-0

DOLLY PARTON

ISBN: 978-1-78603-760-2

BRUCE LEE

ISBN: 978-1-78603-789-3

RUDOLF NUREYEV

ISBN: 978-1-78603-791-6

ZAHA HADID

ISBN: 978-1-78603-745-9

MARY SHELLEY

ISBN: 978-1-78603-748-0

MARTIN LUTHER KING JR.

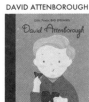

ISBN: 978-0-7112-4567-9

DAVID ATTENBOROUGH

ISBN: 978-0-7112-4564-8

ASTRID LINDGREN

ISBN: 978-0-7112-5217-2

EVONNE GOOLAGONG

ISBN: 978-0-7112-4586-0

BOB DYLAN

ISBN: 978-0-7112-4675-1

ALAN TURING

ISBN: 978-0-7112-4678-2

BILLIE JEAN KING

ISBN: 978-0-7112-4693-5

GRETA THUNBERG

ISBN: 978-0-7112-5645-3

JESSE OWENS

ISBN: 978-0-7112-4583-9

JEAN-MICHEL BASQUIAT
ISBN: 978-0-7112-4580-8

ARETHA FRANKLIN

ISBN: 978-0-7112-4686-7

CORAZON AQUINO

ISBN: 978-0-7112-4684-3

PELÉ

ISBN: 978-0-7112-4573-0

ERNEST SHACKLETON
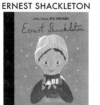
ISBN: 978-0-7112-4571-6

STEVE JOBS
ISBN: 978-0-7112-4577-8

AYRTON SENNA

ISBN: 978-0-7112-4672-0

LOUISE BOURGEOIS

ISBN: 978-0-7112-4690-4

ELTON JOHN

ISBN: 978-0-7112-5840-2

JOHN LENNON

ISBN: 978-0-7112-5767-2

PRINCE

ISBN: 978-0-7112-5439-8

CHARLES DARWIN

ISBN: 978-0-7112-5771-9

CAPTAIN TOM MOORE
ISBN: 978-0-7112-6209-6

HANS CHRISTIAN ANDERSEN

ISBN: 978-0-7112-5934-8

STEVIE WONDER

ISBN: 978-0-7112-5775-7

MEGAN RAPINOE

ISBN: 978-0-7112-5783-2

MARY ANNING

ISBN: 978-0-7112-5554-8

MALALA YOUSAFZAI
ISBN: 978-0-7112-5904-1

ACTIVITY BOOKS

STICKER ACTIVITY BOOK

ISBN: 978-0-7112-6012-2

COLORING BOOK
ISBN: 978-0-7112-6136-5

LITTLE ME, BIG DREAMS JOURNAL

ISBN: 978-0-7112-4889-2